Beyond The Code

Comprehension and Reasoning Skills

3

Nancy Hall

EDUCATORS PUBLISHING SERVICE
Cambridge and Toronto

Printed in Benton Harbor, MI, in April 2021
ISBN 978-0-8388-2403-0

19 20 21 22 PPG 24 23 22 21

Contents

Review of *Beyond The Code 2*

- Remember the words you learned in *Beyond The Code 1* and *2*? Some of them are reviewed below.
- Draw a line from the word to the picture of the word.

head

old   find

news   money

light

Which Words Rhyme?

- Draw a line from the word in the first list to the word that rhymes in the second list. (Remember, words that rhyme are not always spelled the same way.)

know	ever
now	show
never	right
said	how
could	bed
night	would

Introduction to **Kids Need Pets**

- Draw a line to connect the first part of the word to the last part. The first one is done for you. Then read the new words.

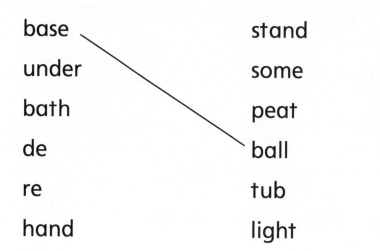

base	stand
under	some
bath	peat
de	ball
re	tub
hand	light

- Now write the last part of the new word next to its meaning. The first part of the word is written for you.

1. a game 2 teams play with a ball and bat = base_____

2. to say over and over = re_____

3. to know what some•thing means = under_____

4. good look•ing = hand_____

5. glad•ness = de_____

6. you sit in it to get clean = bath_____

Words for **Kids Need Pets**

1. **any** = en + E
   Is **any** cake left on the plate?

   Write and spell it: _____

   many = m + **any**
   How **many** kids are in your class?

   Write and spell it: _____

2. **cannot** = can + not
   I **cannot** see the ship.

   Write and spell it: _____

3. **little** = lit + tl
   She has a **little** pet cat.

   Write and spell it: _____

4. **too** = 2
   He had **too** much to eat.

   Write and spell it: _____

5. **maybe** = may + be
   Maybe it will rain.

   Write and spell it: _____

Now read the word list again.

Words for **Kids Need Pets**

• Draw a line from each sentence to the picture it goes with.

Bea **cannot** find her money.

Rex hasn't **any** fish in his bowl.

Sam is **too little** to cross the street by him•self.

Mom says **maybe** we will go to the beach.

How **many** geese are in the nest?

Kids Need Pets

"I want a cat," said Pat to Dad.

"You cannot have a cat, Pat," said Dad.

"A cat has a lot of fuzz!" SKUZZ! SKUZZ!

"I want a dog," said Pat to Dad.

"You cannot have a dog, Pat," said Dad.

"Dogs run and jump up on beds." YUP! YUP!

"I bet I can get a frog," said Pat to Dad.

"You cannot get a frog," said Dad.

"A frog needs a bank of mud and a pond.

A frog is not a pet like a cat or a dog." WOG! WOG!

"I want a goat," said Pat to Dad.

"You cannot have a goat, Pat," said Dad.

"A goat will just eat up your coat." GULP! GULP!

"I want some fish," said Pat to Dad.

"You cannot have fish, Pat," said Dad.

"You have no tank and no cash to get one." SPLASH! SPLASH!

"I want a snake," said Pat to Dad.

"You cannot have a snake, Pat," said Dad.

"A snake will slide and glide and scare us." CRIM! CRIME!

"You cannot have a snake at any time!"

"Oh, man! It's not fair, Dad! I need a pet real bad.
  I need a pet—not many! Just one little one!" Pat told him.
"When you are big and can feed and take care of it,
  then maybe you can get a pet," said Dad.

Pat needs a pet to have at home.
Pat wants a pet to be her own.
But Dad says, "No," and *"No,"* and "NO!"
This makes Pat feel so sad and low.

Pat sits by a tree. She feels so sad.

She just can't understand her dad.

When she picks up her lunch•box and stands up to go,

she sees it! A bug! A pet at long last!

A big bug, her own bug . . . black and fast!

Now Pat can have her own pet at last.

"His name will be Bugs, and Dad will not see him.

I will keep him," thinks Pat. "I will not need to free him."

So off the two go . . . Pat and her black bug!

With the bug in her lunch•box Pat skips home.

But Bugs slips and slides in•side the box.

He just hates that cold, slick box.

So Pat lets Bugs ride in her base•ball cap.

But Bugs gets too hot in that old felt cap!

At home Pat takes her new pet, the bug,

and hides him under her bed . . . so snug!

But Bugs is not a bed•bug . . . in **any** way!

And this spot is much too snug for a bug like Bugs.

Next, Pat gives the bath•tub a try.

But the tub makes Bugs rub his legs side by side.

This makes a soft kind of hum you can't hide.

And Pat fears that Dad may hear and come by.

Pat gives Bugs five drops of milk.

(She thinks that will be good for a black bug to sip.)

But, no, no, no, Bugs will not drink it.

Bugs blinks at Pat . . . then backs up a bit.

Now Pat is so glad to have a pet of her own

that she picks the bug up and gives him a pat and a hug.

But bugs don't want milk or pats or hugs.
And bugs can't stand beds or caps or tubs!
So Bugs nips Pat right on the chin
and then speeds off as fast as the wind!

If you find a hand•some bug, don't pick it up!
Don't take it home or make it your own!
Don't pat it or squeeze it or poke it or keep it.
(Please do as I say, for I'll not re•peat it!)
If you must show your de•light with a hug,
never, never, never hug a big, black bug!

Yes **No**  **Can't Tell**

• Draw the face to show the answer.

1. Did Pat want a pet goat?

2. Did Dad say Pat could have a pet when she is ten?

3. Did Pat plan to set Bugs free the next day?

4. Did Bugs hate to ride in the lunch•box?

5. Was Bugs hand•some?

6. Do bugs like milk?

7. Did a bug make a good pet?

When did Dad say Pat could get a pet?

_____

- -

_____

Opposites

• Draw a line from the word to its opposite.

fast   stand

begin   big

sit   white

black   slow

little   end

13

Draw a big Bugs in the glass. Give him feel•ers and six legs.
Then draw the rest of Pat.

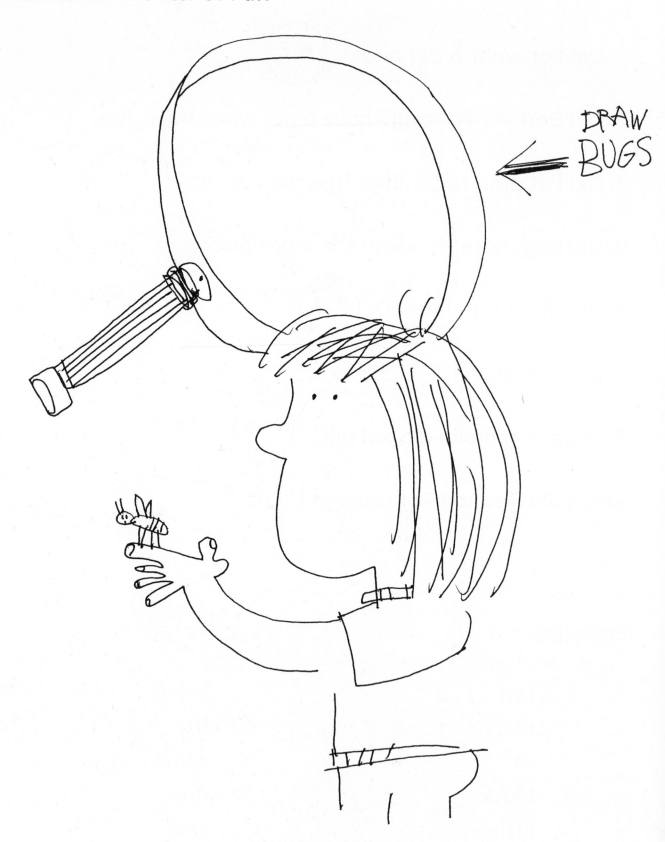

DRAW
BUGS

14

Think About It!

1. Name a kind of pet that Pat did *not* ask for.

2. How are a lunch•box and a book•bag the same?

3. Name a thing you cannot hold in your hand.

4. Name two things that are not fast.

5. Why did Pat need a pet?

6. How do you think Dad feels about pets?

Can You Figure This Out?

Name 2 things that:

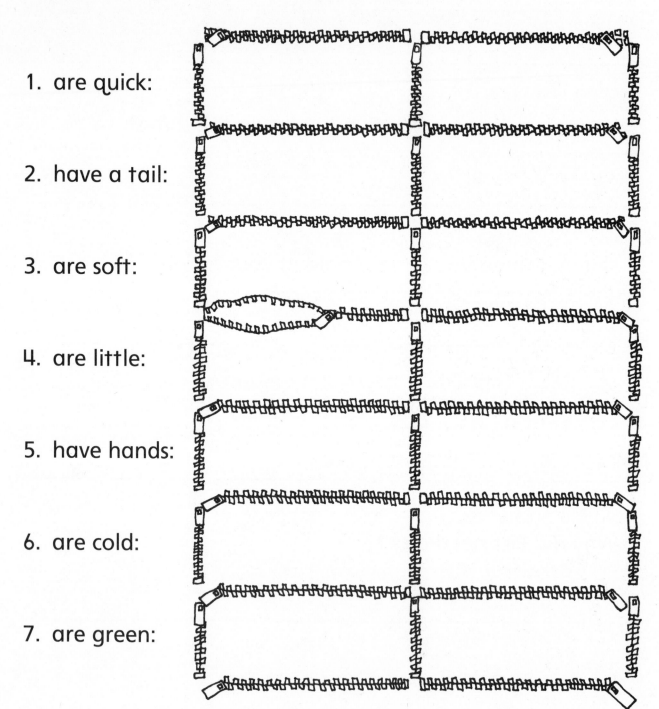

1. are quick:

2. have a tail:

3. are soft:

4. are little:

5. have hands:

6. are cold:

7. are green:

More Review of *Beyond The Code 2*

• Draw a line from the word to the picture of the word.

window   people

spaghetti   door

climb   wagon

• Use the words in the box to finish the sentences below.

says	wants	after
playground	cool	know

1. Mom _____ that I can go to the show with you.

2. I _____ how to spell my last name.

3. The sun was not out; it was a _____, gray day.

4. Let's go to the _____ to swing _____

   school.

5. Little Bo Peep _____ to find her sheep.

Introduction to **What's the Fuss?**

• Circle the part of each group of words that is the same.
  Then read the words out loud.

camp out

with•out

look•out

up•set

sun•set

re•set

her•self

my•self

it•self

speak

weak

squ<u>ea</u>k

real

meal

squ<u>ea</u>l

rain•coat

rain•drop

rain•bow

Words for **What's the Fuss?**

1. **eyes** = I + z

   Close your **eyes** and go to sleep now.

   Write and spell it: _____

2. **moon** =

   I see a full **moon** in the sky.

   Write and spell it: _____

3. **there** = **There** rhymes with *where*.

   There is no room in the wagon.

   Write and spell it: _____

4. **toe** = t + O

   He has a sore **toe**, so he can't walk.

   Write and spell it: _____

5. **wild** = w + I + ld

   Have you seen a **wild** fox?

   Write and spell it: _____

6. **very** = v + air + E

   The fire is **very** hot.

   Write and spell it: _____

Now read the word list again.

Words for **What's the Fuss?**

• Draw a line from each sentence to the picture it goes with.

There are lots of fish in the sea.

The **moon** is like a ball that shines in the sky.

I see the **eyes** of the **wild** skunk.

Fred hit his **toe** on the chair leg.

Jane was **very** glad that she won a prize.

What's the Fuss?

Squeak! Squeal! Scratch! Tap! Mom, Dad, what is that? Is there a wagon with old wheels down in the street? I wake up, but I cannot see a thing. The moon is up, but Mom and Dad are not.

EEK! There is such a fuss near my window. I tip•toe down the stairs and out the door to see. Brave me! What can it be? By the light of the moon I can see the leaves sway. Now the squeal gets so wild I plug my ears, but I stay!

I hear my dad snore from his bed in•side. I try to
shake off sleep and open my eyes wide. Now at last
I can see a bit more. What is that by the back door?

I look and look till I can just make it out. The thing has long wings, little eyes, and small ears. It slides out from under the window where it hides. Its wings flap, and down it glides. Now it is clear: it's a bat! No, there are two bats . . . no, three!

Bats fly so fast that if you blink you could miss them.
They are on the look•out for bugs to have as a meal.
How do they tell when one is near? They can't see the bug;
but they can hear!

I know it is very good to have bats live near your home. They're a big help to people all over the globe. But still I shrink back as they dive down and fly near. And I think to my•self, "Please don't see or hear me here."

Yes **No** **Can't Tell**

• Draw the face to show the answer.

1. Did the kid in the story yell for help?

2. Do bats like to eat bugs that fly?

3. Do bats need big ears to hear well?

4. Are there just two bats on this night?

5. Can bats play hide and seek?

6. Do bats squeal and squeak?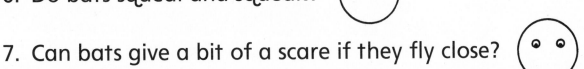

7. Can bats give a bit of a scare if they fly close?

What time of day do bats like to eat?

_____

- -

_____

Opposites

• Draw a line from the word to its opposite.

catch	pull
push	go
moon	throw
wild	tame
wait	sun

Draw wings on the bats as they squeal and squeak at night.

Think About It!

1. How are the sun and moon a·like?

_____

_____

2. Name a thing that can fly fast but is not a bat.

_____

_____

3. Why do bats need good ears?

_____

_____

4. How do you know if it is sun·set?

_____

_____

5. Why did the kid in the story not want the bats to see him?

_____

_____

6. Why is it good to have bats live near your home?

_____

_____

Can You Figure This Out?

• Circle the answer.

1. Which has no legs?   Snake or chair?

2. Which has no eyes?   Tree or king?

3. Which has no hands?   Clock or chick?

4. Which has no color?   Rain•bow or window?

5. Which has no bed?   Fish or dog?

6. Which has no neck?   Plant or sheep?

7. Which has no life?   Stove or deer?

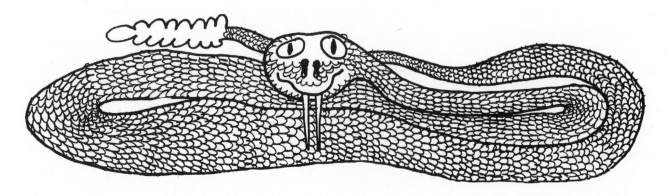

Introduction to **Kal Grows Up and Up**

• Circle the parts of each word group that are the same.
  Then read the words out loud.

there	any•where	cow
where	some•where	now
	no•where	how

• In *Beyond The Code 2* you learned the word *about*. The first letter
  sounds like /u/. Circle the first letter in the words below and then
  read the words out loud.

alike	away
alone	ago
along	agreed
across	asleep

• Circle *be* in each of these words. Then read the words out loud.

begin	become
behave	beside
belong	below

More Introduction to **Kal Grows Up and Up**

• Draw a line to connect the first part of the word with the last part. Then read the new words.

sud   like

dis   fire

six   ner

camp   den

win   look

out   teen

• Now write the last part of the new word next to its meaning. The first part of the word is written for you.

1. someone who wins; the champ = win_____

2. quick; with no hint of what's to come = sud_____

3. to not like a thing at all = dis_____

4. an out•door fire = camp_____

5. it comes after 15 = six_____

6. the way someone looks at life = out_____

What Does It Mean?

A **tall tale** is one that is not _____. It is made up.

Cut-offs are pants that have been _____.

If your **out•look** is not good, you feel _____.

Is an **out•look** the same as a look•out?_____

Words for **Kal Grows Up and Up**

1. **does** = duz

   Does she skate well?

   Write and spell it: _____

   doesn't = duz + nt

   Why **doesn't** Liz want to play?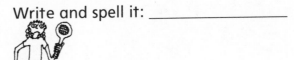

   Write and spell it: _____

2. **shoes** =

   The new **shoes** fit her feet.

   Write and spell it: _____

3. **goes** = **Goes** rhymes with *nose*.

   Chad **goes** to school at nine.

   Write and spell it: _____

4. **school** =

   I read books in **school**.

   Write and spell it: _____

5. **grew** = **Grew** rhymes with *new*.

   The grass **grew** very fast.

   Write and spell it: _____

6. **write** = rite

   Write your name on your paper.

   Write and spell it: _____

Now read the word list again.

Words for **Kal Grows Up and Up**

• Draw a line from each sentence to the picture it goes with.

The **school** bus **goes** down my street.

Can you run fast in your new **shoes**?

The bear **doesn't** know how to **write.**

Does Jake have to walk to **school**?

That pup **grew** very fast!

Kal Grows Up and Up

Kal is a little kid . . . just six years old. But he is very small . . . so small . . . too small. (He is not e•ven as big as his dog, Spike!) Kal's mom frets that he is much too small.

"Why doesn't Kal grow tall?" she asks.

Then all of a sud•den Kal begins to eat and eat.
Mom just can't fill him up. Kal wants to eat all the
time. As he eats more and more, he begins to grow
big . . . very big!

Kal gets so big he can't fit into his jeans. So his
mom makes them cut-offs. But his legs are so long
e•ven the cut-offs don't fit!

Kal's feet get so big they don't fit in his shoes. But Dad's shoes fit him, and Kal likes them a lot. So he slips them on, then off he trots. Dad does not know as he sits and reads the news. (But what will Dad do with•out his shoes?)

Now this tall tale has just begun. There is much more to come!

Kal grows so big he can't fit on his bike. His legs are too long, much to his dis•like. Now Kal has grown as tall as Mom. Where does he fit now? What can he do? Too small, then too big! How come he grew and grew?

Kal is so big . . . too big for six! It's sad when he can't fit in the tub, for now he's a big mess . . . a bit of a grub! You could say that Kal needs a good scrub!

In class Kal is too big to sit at his desk. So he can't write or add or take any tests. You see, Kal is not a bit like the rest.

In fact, Kal is too big to go to school. Kal likes school so much; it's never a bore! But he is too tall to fit in the door. So Kal can go to class no more!

Now Kal can't e•ven fit in his bed. His head sticks up, and his feet stick out. Kal can't get any rest, so his out•look is not the best! As you can see, Kal doesn't fit in! He does not e•ven know **how** to begin!

Mom tells Kal to slow down. Dad says, "Please do not grow!" But Kal cannot stop; he can't e•ven grow slow!

But do you know what?

Kal's legs can run fast. He can kick and throw well. And when he bats he hits a grand slam! On skates he is quick; on a hike he's the lead•er. He can stand on his head; he can hang by his toes. He can catch a ball any•where it goes.

Did you know that Kal can jump over a tall tree? He's also the best when he's in the sea. He can float on his back and blow like a whale. (He just never seems to fail.) Kal can swim all the way across the lake. And blow out a camp•fire with just one puff!

It is just the same with any task or game. (One day Kal may be in the Hall of Fame!)

Kal may not fit in, but he is a win•ner. The kids all
yell, "Let Kal be with me!" "We want Kal on our
home team!" Kal is a champ, as you can see.

The kids all like Kal; they think that he's keen.
(Now I ask, if Kal is this good at six, how will he be
at six•teen?) Kal is BIG and not like the rest. But what
a kid! Kal is the best!

Yes **No** **Can't Tell**

• Draw the face to show the answer.

1. Is Kal in Grade 1 in school?

2. Does Dad take his shoes off when he reads the news?

3. Was Kal's bath•tub very small?

4. Does Kal look like a whale?

5. Can Kal hang by his teeth?

6. Do the kids think Kal is cool?

7. Is this tall tale real?

Name three things Kal can do well.

_____

- -

_____

Opposites

• Draw a line from the word to its opposite.

new	be•low
more	goes
sleep	less
above	wake
comes	old

Draw the tree as Kal jumps over it. Don't for•get to give Kal shoes.

Think About It!

1. How are shoes and socks alike?

_____

_____

2. What can grow very, very big that is not a kid?

_____

_____

3. Why was Kal sad that he could not go to school?

_____

_____

4. Name a thing that is both cold and wet.

_____

_____

5. How are a tall tale and a fib alike?

_____

_____

6. How do you know when you need new shoes?

_____

_____

Can You Figure This Out?

• Some things go together. Each word on the head goes with a word next to the legs. Draw a line to connect the words that go together. The first one is done for you.

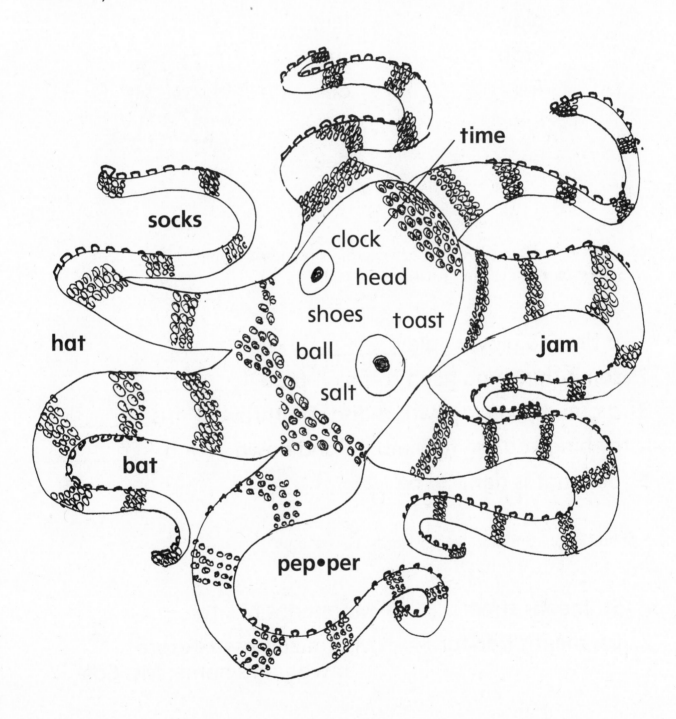

time

socks

clock

head

shoes   toast

hat   ball

salt   jam

bat

pep•per

Introduction to **Day Care for Dogs**

• Draw a line to connect the first part of the word to the last part.
  Then read these new words.

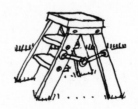

play	lem
prob	time
fris	der
lad	hāve
be	bee

• Now write the last part of the new word next to its meaning.
  The first part of the word is written for you.

1. a time to play = play_____

2. some•thing you need to fix = prob_____

3. a game you play with a disc you throw = fris_____

4. a thing you use to climb up and down = lad_____

5. do what is right = be_____

• Abbreviations are shortcuts for words. For example:

St. means street.   Mr. means Mis•ter.

Dr. means Doc•tor.   Ms. [miz] is used before
                            a woman's name: Ms. Cole

Words for **Day Care for Dogs**

1. **other** = uth + er
   I can't find my **other** shoe.

   Write and spell it: _____

2. **before** = be + 4
   Brush your teeth **before** you go to bed.

   Write and spell it: _____

3. **family** = fam + lee
   My **family** went to the lake last May.

   Write and spell it: _____

4. **chew** = **Chew** rhymes with *new*.
   You must **chew** meat well.

   Write and spell it: _____

5. **hard** = (the opposite of *soft*)
   Some nuts have **hard** shells.

   Write and spell it: _____

6. **together** = to + geth + er
   This tastes good when I mix it all **together**.

   Write and spell it: _____

7. **tired** = tire + d
   She was **tired** after she ran six miles.

   Write and spell it: _____

Now read the word list again.

Words for **Day Care for Dogs**

• Draw a line from each sentence to the picture it goes with.

My **family** likes to shop at the mall.

If it rains we will play ball some **other** day.

Chuck has lost some teeth, and now he can't **chew hard** rolls.

When the bug rubs its legs **together**, it makes a buzz.

We get **tired** when we play soccer **before** school.

50

Day Care for Dogs

"What can I do?" thinks Ms. Keats. Just before school let out three months ago, she got a cute, new pup she calls King Cole. She and King have had such a good time, but next week Ms. Keats must go back to school to teach. King has grown a lot, and now he is too big and play•ful to be left alone. "What can I do about King Cole?" she asks.

The Smith family has the same prob•lem. Last May a black lab pup was left by the front door. For the three kids, Dave, Beth, and Rick, it was fun to look after Rex. They could watch the pup grow. But now the kids must go back to school. Mom and Dad have jobs away from home, and they can't leave Rex alone, for when they do he chews up shoes.

Three miles away Dr. Neal had told his wife, Dr. Rose, "We have no kids, so I think we need a pet." When she agreed they went to the pet store and got a small bull•dog by the name of Cass.

But Cass doesn't like it when no one is at home. She goes wild, tips over the trash, and rips up any•thing she finds. Dr. Rose and Dr. Neal can't bear to put Cass in a pen, so they must try to think what to do.

That very same day they all saw this ad:

DAY CARE FOR DOGS
Does your dog need more play•time than you can give? Is it hard for your dog to be alone all day? For just $15 a day we can help you and your dog. Call us at 423-DOGS.

When the people rang up they were told that before a dog can go to day care it must pass a test to see if it gets along with other dogs. King Cole, Rex, and Cass all pass the test.

At 8 o'clock the school bus comes by to pick up the dogs. The bus makes just three stops. The Smiths drive Rex to the Main St. bus stop and wave good•bye to him as he hops on the bus. A man on the bus shows Rex to his seat and puts his seat belt on for him. (Rex likes to go to school on the bus, just like the kids.)

Ms. Keats waits at the next stop with King. She blows him a kiss as he climbs up the steps of the bus.

"See you at 5 o'clock, King. Have a good day!" calls Ms. Keats, and then she heads for school, too. Last of all, the bus picks up Cass, the bull•dog, along with three other big dogs at the Pine St. bus stop.

Lots of tails wag as the dogs on the bus greet them.
Each dog has a lunch bag with his own treat for snack
time. Rex likes bones, while Cass wants beef bits, and
King brings fish sticks.

All the dogs sit still on the bus. They never fuss over
where to sit or which dog will sit next to them. They
never yip or run up and down in the bus. They know
they must be•have on the school bus.

When the school day begins, the dogs all meet together to run about and check each other out. Then they are sent off in twos or threes for more play•time. Will they play Chase the Ball or Catch the Fris•bee to•day? The dogs meet, greet, and play the day away.

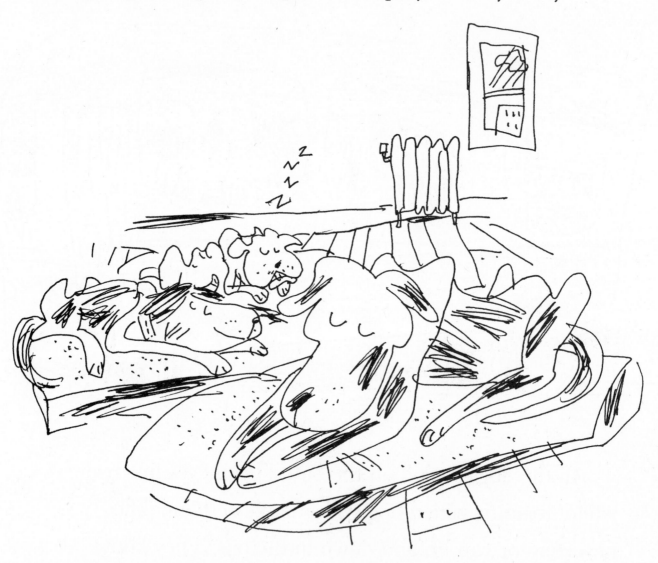

After lunch it is time to rest. Each dog has its own bed from home to sleep on. (Some dogs snore as they nap!)

When the dogs get back from day care at five P.M., they are tired, but they are glad to be home. They all seem to know that no mat•ter what your family is like, it is just right!

Yes **No** **Can't Tell**

• Draw the face to show the answer.

1. Is it hard to leave some pets alone all day?

2. Did Ms. Keats teach school?

3. Did all the dogs on the bus put on seat belts?

4. Do many people own dogs?

5. Did the dogs have to take a math test?

6. Do all dogs like to play fris•bee?

7. Is each family the same?

Why can't some dogs be left at home alone?

_____

- -

_____

Opposites

• Draw a line from the word to its opposite.

hard	weak
together	soft
strong	after
before	night
day	alone

Draw more of the dogs at nap time.
Give them each a dog bed.

Think About It!

1. Name some•thing you can eat that has skin.

_____

- -

_____

2. How are stairs and a lad•der the same?

_____

- -

_____

3. What is both soft and wild?

_____

- -

_____

4. How do dogs say hello?

_____

- -

_____

5. How can you tell that it is about to rain?

_____

- -

_____

6. Why do some kids fuss over where they sit on a bus?

_____

- -

_____

Can You Figure This Out?

Name 2 things that:

1. you can chew:

2. can grow:

3. are very cute:

4. are hard:

5. have toes:

6. you can zip:

7. you do in
   school:

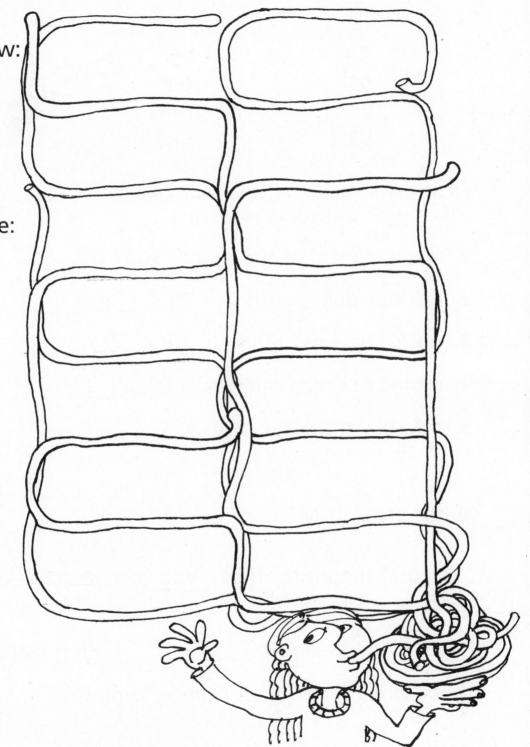

Introduction to **A Fish That Can Fly!**

• Draw a line to connect the first part of the word with the last part.
  Then read the new words.

sis   er

sup   per

old   ter

in   fish

blue   side

• Now write the last part of the new word next to its meaning.
  The first part is written for you.

1. the last meal of the day = sup_____

2. not out•doors = in_____

3. not as new as before = old_____

4. a blue or green sea fish = blue_____

5. a family mem•ber = sis_____

What Does It Mean?

"To cast" means to throw. You cast your fish line into
the _____.

"To reel in" means to _____ in a fish with a line.

If you are "down in the dumps," you feel _____.

Words for **A Fish That Can Fly!**

1. **learn** = l + er + n
   We **learn** to read in school.

   Write and spell it: _____

2. **young** = yung (the opposite of *old*)
   A **young** goat is a kid.

   Write and spell it: _____

3. **blue** = Blue rhymes with 2.
   Where did the **blue** sky go?

   Write and spell it: _____

4. **love** = luv
   I **love** my pet dog.

   Write and spell it: _____

5. **water** =
   Water falls from the sky as rain.

   Write and spell it: _____

6. **warm** = the opposite of *cool*
   The water is not **warm** yet.

   Write and spell it: _____

Now read the word list again.

Words for **A Fish That Can Fly!**

• Draw a line from each sentence to the picture it goes with.

When the **water** is **warm,** I will take a bath.

I like to sail my boat on the **blue** sea.

Chip **learns** to walk at last.

Joan is very **young** to go on the train alone.

I **love** to skate at the rink.

A Fish That Can Fly!

Seth doesn't want to go to the shack. In fact, he can't stand the shack! To get there you must drive down a long road past a sand beach where the waves are too big and the wind is too brisk. The shack is a lot like a camp with no heat and no lights. You must bring water to drink and jump in the cold sea to get clean.

But Seth's sis•ter, Dale, loves to be at the shack. (So does Mom!) Dale has such fun there, but she can swim and Seth cannot! Dale runs in the sand, hunts for shells, and rides the waves. She doesn't care if a wave hits her and dumps her over. Smack!

As the sun sets at the shack, the kids both yell, "Let's eat!" Mom lights the gas lamp so they can see, and then she puts the hot dogs on the grill.

But at sup•per Seth does not eat. The hot dogs are still cold in•side, the rolls are stale and dry, and the milk tastes odd. Even the chips have no crunch!

"Yuck, the shack is not for me," sniffs Seth to him•self so no one can hear. "If I were at home I'd have a warm meal of spaghetti and cheese! Yum!"

At night the shack feels cold and damp, and so do the bunks! But Dale smiles as she flops on her bunk. "Isn't this the best? I love it here! Don't you, Seth?"

"Yup, but I'm cold," whines Seth.

"We have warm down bags so we'll be snug in a bit," she tells him. (Seth does not think so. He dreams of home, his soft, warm bed, and TV!)

WHUFF! A gust of wind blows out the gas lamp. Now it is so black! Dale grins and yells, "This is such fun!"

"I want to go home," thinks Seth, but Mom and Dale can't hear him. Seth pulls his down bag up over his ears. He knows he must not sulk or be down in the dumps. Seth blinks back the tears. "Do I have to spend nine more days out here?" he sniffs.

The next day the two kids go with Mom over the
dunes to the beach. Mom takes her fish pole and reel
and a small clam for bait. She casts her line and pulls it
in and casts it one more time. Then Seth sees a tug on
Mom's line. She reels it in slow and hard, and there at
last in the waves is a big, big blue•fish! Look at it flap!
What a fish!

Now Seth wants to catch a fish, too. But he is too weak to cast his line from the shore and too little to row a boat out where the fish are. Mom says he's too young to fish.

"You must grow up and learn to swim before you can fish," she adds.

"I am not too little! I am not too young or too weak," he wails at the top of his lungs. "It's not fair! I want to catch a fish, just like you! I'll never learn to swim!"

Mom feels bad for Seth. She knows that he doesn't like to be at the shack with no heat and no lights and no TV. So after lunch she hops in her truck and drives down the beach road to the store. She needs to get some milk and a can of beans. (But most of all, she wants to get a treat for Seth.)

When Mom gets back she has a gift for Seth . . . a big kite in the shape of a fish, and it's blue!

"This is the best fish ever, and it's mine!" he yells as he skips off to the beach and lets it fly up in the sky. "Look, Dale! See my blue•fish? Isn't it cool? Now I've got a big fish on my line, just like Mom!"

Seth holds onto the string as the kite soars up, up, up in the sky over his and Dale's heads . . . so big and so blue and so grand. The kids stand and stare in de•light!

"Well," thinks Seth, "maybe the shack isn't so bad after all."

Yes **No** **Can't Tell**

• Draw the face to show the answer.

1. Does Mom make good meals at the shack?

2. Do Mom and the kids build a camp•fire to get warm?

3. Does Seth want to catch fish?

4. Will Seth's mom teach him how to fish some•day?

5. Is Dale old•er than Seth?

6. Can Seth eat his fish for sup•per?

7. Does Seth like the shack at the end of the week?

How old do you think Seth is? How old will you be next year?

_____

_____

Opposites

• Draw a line from the word to its opposite.

young	fresh
give	hate
warm	take
stale	old
love	cool

Draw what Seth has on his line.

Think About It!

1. Name some•thing you can do with cash.

2. How do kites fly?

3. Name a thing that can blow out that is not a gas lamp.

4. Why do fish need water?

5. Why does Dale like the shack?

6. Would Seth like the shack if it had TV?
   Tell why or why not.

Can You Figure This Out?

Name some•thing that:

1. you can eat that has a crust _____

2. is big and made of glass _____

3. has skin that you can peel _____

4. you can eat that has seeds _____

5. is cold and falls from the sky _____

6. is sweet and you lick it _____

7. you can sit on, and it has a back _____

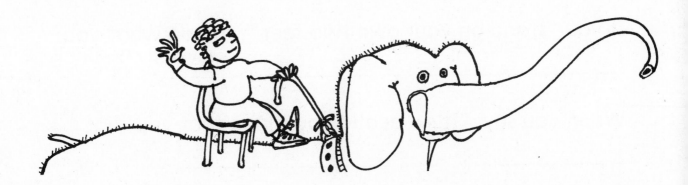

Introduction to **Kate and Her Ten-Speed Bike**

• Draw a line to connect the first part of the word with the last part.
  Then read the new words.

skate	way
mis	board
drive	take
book	ner
din	case

• Now write the last part of the new word next to its meaning.
  The first part is written for you.

1. the meal at the end of the day = din_____

2. a low, flat board with wheels = skate_____

3. where you drive into your home = drive_____

4. a place to keep books = book_____

5. some•thing that you didn't mean to do or say =
   mis_____

What Does It Mean?

If you "stand on your own two feet," you do what you

_____.

When you say, "It's a deal!" you mean that you

_____.

Words for **Kate and Her Ten-Speed Bike**

1. **apples** =

   Apples are good to eat.

   Write and spell it: _____

2. **won't** = **Won't** rhymes with *don't*.

   I **won't** cry if I miss the bus.

   Write and spell it: _____

3. **clothes** = cl + O + ths

   Coats and pants and socks are **clothes**.

   Write and spell it: _____

4. **wear** = w + air

   Dee **wears** a long cape.

   Write and spell it: _____

5. **instead** = in + sted

   I don't like beets; I eat beans **instead**.

   Write and spell it: _____

6. **knew** = new

   I **knew** all the words on the test.

   Write and spell it: _____

Now read the word list again.

Words for **Kate and Her Ten-Speed Bike**

• Draw a line from each picture to the sentence it goes with.

I can't call you. Will you call me **instead**?

Steff picks **apples** to make money.

We **won't** play when Mom needs help.

Jake **wears** his new **clothes** to school.

Jess **knew** how to do a flip.

Kate and Her Ten-Speed Bike

Last May when Kate was nine years old, she got
a new ten-speed bike. Dad said he would help her learn
to ride it. She never fell off her bike, and in no time at all
she could ride well! Kate is very tall and strong for nine.

Kate knows what she likes and doesn't like. She won't wear a dress; she wears pants instead. She doesn't like pink; she likes red. She won't put bows or clips in her hair or paint her nails. She likes cool hats, but she won't wear frills. Kate stands on her own two feet and does what seems best to her!

Kate and Dad like to spend time together and chat. One day as they talk Dad asks Kate what she would like next May when she is ten. Kate thinks and thinks. "This is hard," she says, "but I think I want a pet white rat. No dolls, please! No games, no rings, no clothes! No, thank you! Just a white rat!"

Dad smiles and says, "We'll see."

In her free time Kate likes to climb and jump off walls and throw rocks at tin cans. She likes snakes and toads and snails. She likes to fish and play soccer and glide on her skate•board. But best of all, Kate likes to ride fast on her ten-speed bike.

Last week Kate came home late from a ride on the bike trail with her pals. Mom and Dad had told her that she must be home before six o'clock when the family eats sup•per. It was now 6:15 P.M. In her rush Kate left her bike in the drive•way.

That night when Dad drove down the drive•way in his pick•up truck to go to the store, he didn't see Kate's bike. CRUNCH! Too late!

Kate let out a scream. "Oooo! My bike!" The bike was a mess! The frame was bent, the tires were flat, and the seat was split. You couldn't tell it was ever a bike! Kate began to cry. "I need my bike! What will I do?"

Kate knew the crash was her mis•take, not Dad's. But Dad felt bad, too. What could he do to help Kate?

"I'll tell you what," Dad said. "I feel bad that I was the one to run over your bike, so I'll pay for some of the cost of a new one. But you still must save $50 on your own."

"Thanks a lot, Dad. That's a big help," Kate said.

Now Kate must think of some ways to make a lot of cash so she can get a new bike fast.

"I could do chores for people on our street," she thinks. "Maybe I could rake leaves or pick up apples off the grass or go to the store for people? I sure hope some•one will hire me," Kate frets.

The next day Mom tells Kate that she will give her $5.00 to clean out the shed. The shed is a mess, but Kate likes to be a mess and wear old clothes, so she says, "OK, Mom, it's a deal! Thanks!"

"What good luck! Now I'll have $5.00," thinks Kate as she throws out all kinds of trash . . . old paint cans and old tires, bug spray and plant spray and window spray, old rugs and tubs and pails with holes.

That night Dad says that he will pay Kate 50¢ each
week if she will take the trash cans out to the road for
pick-up. (Kate is glad to do this chore, too.)

"It sure helps to be strong," she thinks to her•self.
"At this rate I'll have a new bike in no time . . . maybe
before May. But if not, maybe I'll ask for a new bike,
instead of a pet rat!"

Yes **No** **Can't Tell**

• Draw the face to show the answer.

1. Does Kate like to dress up and go out?

2. Does Dad like the way Kate thinks?

3. Was Kate late for din•ner?

4. Did Kate's dad drive a taxi?

5. Did Kate blame Dad when she had no bike?

6. Is Kate's dad a kind man?

7. Do people on the street hire Kate to do jobs?

Tell one thing Kate throws out when she cleans the shed.

_____

_____

Opposites

• Draw a line from the word to its opposite.

open	spend
blame	bad luck
save	mean
kind	shut
good luck	praise

Draw more of Kate and her bent bike.

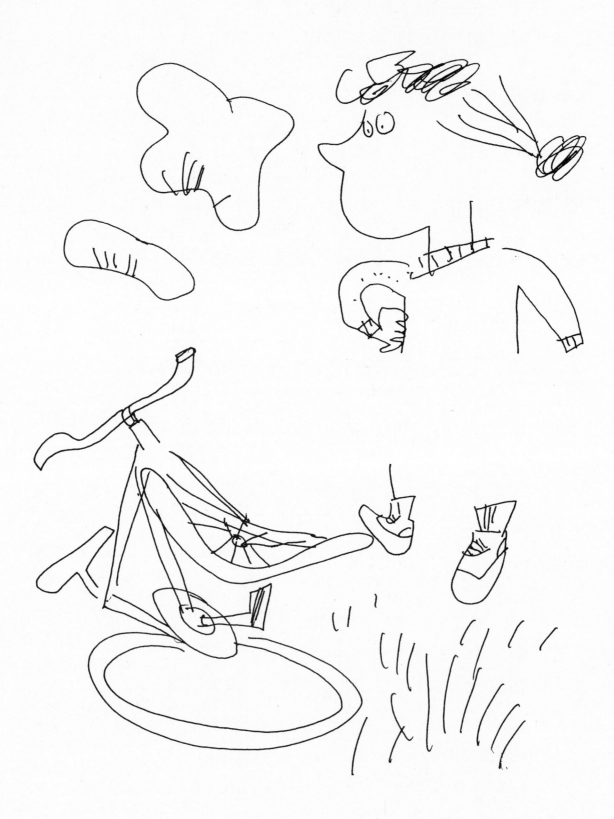

Think About It!

1. What can be bent that is not a bike?

2. How are an apple and a peach the same?

3. Name a job you can do by your•self.

4. How are a skate•board and a bike the same?

5. How much money did Kate have by the end of the week?

6. How do you know when a pal feels bad?

Can You Figure This Out?

• Write the name for all the items on each line. The first is done for you.

1. oak   pine   wil•low   elm   = All <u>trees</u>

2. deer   fox   sheep   pig   = All _____

3. pants   coat   jeans   vest   = All _____

4. desk   chair   book•case   bed   = All _____

5. green   red   blue   pink   = All _____

6. plum   apple   lime   peach   = All _____

7. nine   two   six   three   = All _____

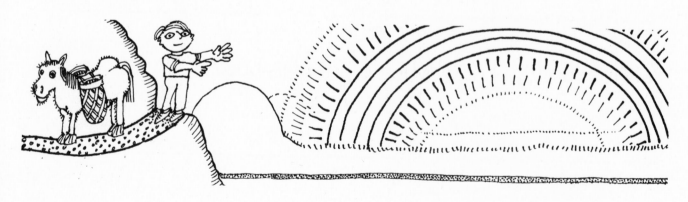

Words Introduced in *Beyond the Code 3*

any	hard	tired
apples	instead	toe
before	knew	together
blue	learn	too
cannot	little	very
chew	love	warm
clothes	many	water
does	maybe	wear
doesn't	moon	wild
eyes	other	won't
family	school	write
goes	shoes	young
grew	there	